Margaret Mead

Bringing World Cultures Together

Michael Pollard

BLACKBIRCH PRESS, INC.

WOODBRIDGE, CONNECTICUT

Published by Blackbirch Press, Inc.
260 Amity Road
Woodbridge, CT 06525
web site: http://www.blackbirch.com
e-mail: staff@blackbirch.com

First published in Great Britain by Exley Publications Ltd., Chalk Hill, Watford, 1992.
© Exley Publications Ltd.
© Michael Pollard

10 9 8 7 6 5 4 3 2

Photo Credits
Cover: CORBIS/Jack Fields.
Courtesy Department of Library Services American Museum of Natural History: 40 (Photo P.E. Logan),
50; The Bettman Archive: 47; Black Star/Colorific!: 60; Compix: 11; Sally and Richard Greenhill: 28;
Robert Harding Picture Library: 6, 7 (top), 42, 43 (top), 52; Hulton Price Picture Company/The Bettman
Archive: 23; The Hutchison Library: 7 (below left and right), 14, 20 (both), 29 (below), 32 (both), 35,
43 (below), 49; Courtesy of the Institute for Intercultural Studies, Inc., New York: 4, 9, 10, 17 (below),
19, 26, 31, 36–37, 39, 45 (both), 59; ZEFA: 17 (top), 24, 25, 29 (top), 56 (both), 57.

Printed in China

Library of Congress Cataloging-in-Publication Data
Pollard, Michael, 1931–
    Margaret Mead: Bringing world cultures together / by Michael Pollard.
        p. cm.—(Giants of science)
    Includes bibliographical references and index.
    Summary: Examines the life of the noted anthropologist who worked to help people
all over the world understand each other's cultures.
    ISBN 1-56711-327-3
    1. Mead, Margaret, 1901–1978—Juvenile literature. 2. Women anthropologists—
United States—Biography—Juvenile literature. 3. Ethnology—Melanasia—Juvenile literature.
4. Melanasia—Social life and customs—Juvenile literature. [1. Mead, Margaret, 1901–1978.
2. Anthropologists. 3. Women—Biography.] I. Title. II. Series.
GN21.M36P65 1999   98–47864
306'.092—dc21   CIP
[b]   AC

Contents

What Makes Us Who We Are?

Where do we get our ideas of what's right or what's wrong, fair or unfair, beautiful or ugly? Are we born with them, or do we get them from our parents and the people around us?

These are the questions that scientists who study the way people behave have been asking for nearly 150 years. In 1859, the British scientist Charles Darwin published his famous book, *On the Origin of Species*, which introduced the idea of "natural selection." With humans, as with all living things, Darwin wrote, the healthier and more successful specimens survived and bred while the weaker ones died out. If there were more strong specimens than weak ones, the specimens grew in number. If not, they began to disappear, or become extinct. In other words, the ability to survive was passed on from parents to children.

It was not long before scientists were wondering whether other things could be passed on in this way. Could it be that there were families in which criminal behavior was passed down from parents to children in the same way as the ability to survive? Some people went even further. What about kindness, or good manners, or bad temper?

There is no easy answer. It often seems that children have the good or bad habits of their parents. But, were they born with those habits, or did they pick them up by imitation? How much do we copy the way other people around us behave, or the

Opposite: *Margaret Mead (on the left) photographed on her first field trip in Samoa in 1925. She is with Fa'amotu, a Samoan chief's daughter who introduced her to local food and customs.*

people we see in films or on television? Behavioral scientists still argue about these questions today.

In the 1920s these arguments were a major focus in the behavioral sciences. In North America and Europe, the concept of free education for all people had been introduced more than fifty years before. It was expected to lead to a better, less violent society—but that hadn't happened. Was there, some people asked, something wrong with the way children were educated—and if so, was this because no one understood how children learn?

Nature vs. Nurture

During the 1920s, there was also an outbreak of concern about the actions and attitudes of rebellious youth. Public worries on the topic were not new, but they had increased because of the potential

Above, left and opposite: *Decorating their bodies is one way in which people of many cultures express their identity, and sometimes their status.*

influence of the movies and radio (which were relatively new forms of media) on young people. One question that was being asked was whether American parents were raising their children in a way that made them reckless and rebellious as teenagers, or whether some children were simply born rebels. Today, many share the same worries about the influence of television, videos, rock music, and the internet. But no one has been able to prove that the media affects the way people behave.

"Nature vs. nurture" is another way to describe this question. Some people say "nature" (heredity) is the most important factor in someone's character and the way he or she behaves. They believe that children inherit these characteristics from their parents and their grandparents in the same way as they receive their physical characteristics. Those who believe in "nurture" (environment) say that the influence of the family and the outside world is the most important factor in determining how a person behaves.

Anthropology

The nature vs. nurture question is of great interest to anthropologists. Anthropology is the study of humans as a species, and anthropologists are concerned with how different types of people have evolved both physically and culturally. For example, why are the pygmies of Central Africa so small and the aborigines of Australia so tall? How has their environment affected their development? Anthropologists are interested in how groups of people—societies—relate to their surroundings. They study how organized societies make sense of the world through family and relationships, religion, language, and the arts. And they try to understand the way in which families and communities work.

One of the scientists in the 1920s who was interested in the nature vs. nurture discussion was Professor Franz Boas, head of the Department of Anthropology at Columbia University in New York. One of his brightest students was a young woman named Margaret Mead.

Woman Pioneer

Born on December 16, 1901, Margaret Mead had lived a sheltered, middle-class life. Her father was a university professor. Her mother was a social-minded woman who often volunteered for good causes. By the time she was an adult, Margaret still had never been to a "foreign" country, and spoke no foreign languages. She had never traveled by boat, or even stayed in a hotel. In all her life, she had never spent a whole day on her own! Furthermore, she had gotten married as a student. Her husband, Luther Cressman, intended to make his career in the Church.

By 1925, Margaret, age twenty-three, had a master's degree in psychology. She was about to receive her doctorate in anthropology, and was ready to start researching topics she had studied for so long. Anthropology is a science where real work must be done "in the field," living closely with the people being studied. Margaret's main subject of study was the people of Polynesia, in the South Pacific. This requirement, however, presented Franz Boas with a problem.

Margaret was determined to continuing studying the culture of Polynesia. Civilization was reaching out to the islands, and soon their customs and way of life would vanish forever. Margaret wanted to observe and record these characteristics before it was too late.

Boas was nervous. He did not know if he could he take responsibility for giving this young woman

> "I was always glad that I was a girl. I cannot remember ever wanting to be a boy. It seems to me this is because of the way I was treated by my parents. I was a wanted child, and when I was born I was the kind of child my parents wanted."
>
> –Margaret Mead,
> from her autobiography
> *Blackberry Winter*

Margaret with her brother Richard. Margaret was the eldest of five children.

permission to travel half-way around the world. The islands she wanted to study—the Tuamotu Islands in French Polynesia—were among the most remote in the world, with only rare outside contacts. She might encounter dangerous animals, deadly disease, and even cannibals.

Today, it is not unusual for a woman to travel around the world. In the 1920s however, it was almost unheard of for a woman to travel alone. It was almost as unusual for a woman—especially a married woman—to plan a professional career. In those days, married women were expected to settle down, make a home, and have children.

Boas suggested that Margaret make a study of Native American Indian culture instead. This would be just as interesting, it could be done in a setting that was much less dangerous, and it was closer to home. The Indian reservation also had good communications with local governments if anything were to go wrong.

Margaret, age twenty-four, just before her departure to Samoa. At a conference of anthropologists in Toronto, Canada, a year before, she had made her decision to start field work as soon as she could.

Wanderlust

In may have also been in Franz Boas's mind that a period of local field work in the United States would cure Margaret of her wanderlust. He thought, perhaps, that she would choose a university-based career instead. But, Margaret insisted that American Indian culture, as Boas suggested, had already been spoiled by contact with white Americans. The changes she wanted to study were already over for the Native American Indians. In the South Pacific, change had not arrived, or had only just begun. She wanted to go where an old culture still lived on, to a place that had not been invaded by modern ideas.

Franz Boas knew that Margaret was a brilliant student who deserved to be given a chance to make a name for herself. He encouraged her to

Fishing was—and still is—a vital industry in Samoa. In this fishing village, the nets are hung out to dry.

research a subject that was very much in the news—the way teenagers behave. She wanted to make a wider study—to observe what happens in a culture when civilization brings change. This idea was to be her lifelong interest.

Boas and his prized student accepted a compromise. She was not interested in studying the American Indians, but if Boas would let her go somewhere else in the South Pacific, she would not insist on Tuamotu. She also agreed to study the way adolescents behave—especially girls—as he had suggested.

Off to Samoa

After some searching, a suitable place was found— Samoa, a group of South Pacific islands about 1,000 miles (1,609 kilometers) south of the equator. Discovered in the eighteenth century, the islands had become very important trading posts.

Later, they became ports of call for steamships to take on fuel and other supplies.

By 1925, the group of islands had become divided in two. Western Samoa, today an independent state, was administered by New Zealand. The eastern half, American Samoa, was (and still is) officially a United States territory. The U. S. Navy had a large base there, with a hospital and a radio station. This was located at Pago Pago on the island of Tutuila.

Access to the American base was the reason that Boas finally agreed to let Margaret work there. If she found herself in any trouble, he reasoned, she would be able to turn to the navy for help. Also, there was regular passenger service to Pago Pago every three weeks, and civilians could send or receive cable messages through the radio station. So on August 31, 1925, Margaret Mead arrived in Samoa. She sailed aboard the *SS Sonoma* after a 3,000 mile (4,828 kilometer) voyage from Hawaii.

Only the Basics

A scientist going on such an expedition today would travel in a group that would include specialists in many different disciplines. They would take a large variety of equipment, including emergency medical supplies, measuring instruments, storage for samples, laptop computers, mobile phones, tape recorders, film, video and still cameras, and film lighting.

Margaret's equipment was far more basic: apart from personal luggage, she brought pencils, notebooks, a camera, and a spare pair of glasses. And she was alone. There would be no chance to discuss her research with anyone—except in letters to Franz Boas and colleagues.

In those days, scientists going to work in the field received no training in methods of observing and recording their findings. No one asked them whether they could stand the loneliness of field work, or how they would cope with possible danger. "Many who are now professors teach their students as their professors taught them," Margaret Mead wrote later, "and if young field workers do not give up in despair, go mad, ruin their health, or die, they do, after a fashion, become anthropologists. But it is a wasteful system, a system I have no time for."

Later in life, Margaret spent a great deal of time training field workers, and helping them to live with the problems they might encounter.

Despite the occasional ships, the Pacific Islands were quite remote in the days before scheduled air service. People in North America and Europe, however, knew a great deal about them. Sailors, missionaries, and explorers had brought back reports of life on the islands. More recently, "the South Seas"—as the southern Pacific was then generally called—had become a place of romantic pilgrimage for many European writers and artists. The Scottish novelist Robert Louis Stevenson lived in Samoa for seven years, and died there. He wrote three books about his experiences on the island.

A popular picture of Polynesians had emerged—simple, friendly people with gracious movements and smiling faces. The English poet, Robert Brooke, who had also lived on Samoa, had described the natives as "the loveliest people in the world, moving and running and dancing like gods and goddesses."

First Impressions

Margaret's first impression upon her arrival at Pago Pago was one of disappointment. The port was noisy with naval aircraft and ship's bands played ragtime music. She was depressed to see how the

U. S. Navy had already introduced American culture and values to the Samoans. The women were dressed, not in the traditional costumes, but in "various hideous striped American stuffs." She felt ashamed of her own country's seemingly corruptive influence on these people.

Over the next few weeks, Margaret visited most of the villages on Tutuila. The ones on bus routes, she found, had been "very much influenced by American goods and American visitors and do not present a typical picture of the original culture." None of the villages had enough teenage girls to make a suitable group for research.

"Because of these disadvantages," she wrote to Boas, "I have decided to go to Ta'u, one of three small islands in the Manu'a group about 100 miles [161 kilometers] from here." There, she explained, she would be able to live with the only white family on the island.

Edward Holt was a U. S. Navy man in charge of the dispensary on Ta'u. He lived in a European-style house with his wife Ruth and their children. There was a spare room for Margaret, and a small house nearby where she could interview the Samoan girls from Ta'u's four villages. In November, having struggled to learn the Samoan language, Margaret set out for Ta'u, where she was to spend the next six months.

The young anthropologist immediately felt more cheerful once she was in Ta'u, though the climate was much hotter. Ta'u proved, as she'd been told, "much more primitive and unspoiled than any other part of Samoa." Soon she was observing and recording Polynesian dances and spending time with native families.

By January, Margaret reported that "gradually I am becoming part of the community." She had learned how to obtain information from the villagers.

....

"There is no way of knowing in advance what the people will be like or even what they will look like. There may be photographs of them, but by the time one arrives they may look different.... One doesn't know where one will live or what there will be to eat or whether it will turn out a good thing to have rubber boots, mosquito boots, sandals that keep one's feet cool, or woollen socks to absorb the sweat."

—Margaret Mead, from her autobiography *Blackberry Winter*

....

Sitting down with them and asking questions involved a ritual of exchanging small gifts. The Samoans gave Margaret shells and flowers, and her gifts were writing paper, envelopes, needles, and thread. She also became a "fixer" for the village people, writing letters for them, obtaining things they wanted from the navy store, and taking photographs for them.

It was an eventful six months. Soon after her arrival, a hurricane devastated the village where she was living. Visits to the other villages involved wading for miles in mud up to her knees. There were mosquitoes everywhere.

Margaret carried out her research in the spare house near the dispensary. She interviewed the village girls, tested their intelligence, and recorded their experiences and family background.

Confusion and Uncertainty

When she returned to Pago Pago on her way home in May 1926, she had collected a large quantity of information about the lives of the young people of Ta'u. Her time and experience in Ta'u made her question some of the beliefs she held as a typical young American woman. Before she went to Samoa, for example, she would not have doubted that it was a good thing to send the village children to school. Now, she saw that the time spent at school could actually cause problems.

Traditionally, it was the six- and seven-year-old girls who looked after the babies of the family, while the boys ran errands and saw to many households tasks, like lighting fires and cleaning lamps. When the children went to school for most of the day, the households became completely disorganized. When the children were home, family life ran like clockwork. The daily running of the house obviously depended on help from the children.

Above: *Among the Mundugumor, and other New Guinea peoples, the men met in their own ceremonial houses, called House Tamburans.*

Left: *Paulo was one of the children of the chief's household where Margaret stayed soon after arriving in Samoa.*

Like Minds

Margaret's voyage home was by way of Australia and Europe. She planned to meet her husband Luther in France. They were going to spend some vacation time together before returning to the United States.

One of the passengers on the voyage from Australia on the *SS Chitral* was a young New Zealand psychologist, Reo Fortune. He was on his way to England to take up a scholarship at Cambridge University. They spent most of their time together comparing ideas and sharing field work experiences.

By the time the *SS Chitral* reached Europe, Reo and Margaret had fallen in love.

At first, Margaret seemed to ignore the obvious. In Europe, she allowed Luther to show her the sights and tell her about his year as a tourist. But her thoughts continued to revolve around her months in Samoa. She remembered the intense conversations with Reo during those weeks at sea. Slowly, she realized how different her interests, view of life, and depth of experience were from her husband's.

"Coming of Age in Samoa"

Back in New York, Margaret Mead began to write an account of her field work, which she titled *Coming of Age in Samoa*. At the same time, Luther started a new career as a lecturer.

As Margaret wrote her book, she felt more and more uncertain about her future. Her marriage was not as fulfilling as she had hoped. Meanwhile, Cambridge University had not worked out for Reo Fortune and he was planning to do field research in the South Pacific. On a visit to Reo in Germany in the summer of 1927, Margaret agreed to marry him and join him in New Guinea if they could arrange to fund the expedition. Then she returned to New York to say goodbye to Luther.

There had already been one disappointment for Margaret. To have work published is all-important to an academic researcher, but despite Boas's support, the first draft of *Coming of Age in Samoa* had been turned down by Harper, a leading American publisher. Recovering swiftly from this blow, she sent a draft to another publisher, William Morrow, who was just setting up his business. He agreed to take it if she would add three chapters explaining what her findings meant for Americans concerned about young peoples' behavior.

Events were now moving quickly in Margaret's life. Reo had obtained a grant and had already started work in New Guinea. Margaret had applied for, and eventually got, a fellowship to fund a year's work there. Her plan was to study very

The success of Margaret's early field work was due largely to her ability to join with children in their games and everyday activities. She was delighted to find in Manus, New Guinea, that it was "a paradise for children. They have no work except to run errands and that involves paddling in the water." There was plenty of time for them to play and for Margaret to study them. Here, she is decorating their hair with strands of scarlet ribbon.

Above: *In Sierre Leone, Africa, children's faces are painted white to mark their change from childhood into adolescence.*

Right: *The son of an Indian noble rides in front of the people.*

young children. Meanwhile, she was devising and making test material to use in her work—as she spent time arranging her divorce. And, in the middle of it all, she also had to write the three extra chapters for William Morrow. At last, late in the summer of 1928, a tired but excited Margaret set off for New Guinea to join her future husband.

Coming of Age in Samoa was still at the printing plant when she left and, in those days before air mail, it was many months before Margaret learned that her book was actually a best seller. In fact, it was such a success that William Morrow ordered a second printing right away.

"Age of Maximum Ease"

Coming of Age in Samoa is a detailed study of the sexual and family customs of teenage girls on the islands, the way Margaret saw them. It contained many picturesque descriptions of the ritual songs and dances, costumes and ornaments of the villagers. But there were unavoidable gaps in Margaret's accounts of life in Samoa. She had spent only ten weeks learning the language. Some of her communication must have been rough. In addition, as a woman, she was not allowed to attend the all-male meetings where political, religious, and economic matters were discussed. So, although she found out how families worked, she discovered little about the workings of the wider community. Later in her career, some of these shortcomings were to bring her criticism.

After the hurricane on Ta'u, all the efforts of the villagers were concentrated on re-building their ruined homes. Many social ceremonies and rituals that Margaret expected to attend had been cancelled. As a result, more of Margaret's information came from the girls she interviewed than from actual observation of the village events.

"We feel grateful to Miss Mead for having undertaken to identify herself so completely with Samoan youth that she gives us a lucid and clear picture of the joys and difficulties encountered by the young individual in a culture so entirely different from our own.... Much of what we ascribe to human nature is no more than a reaction to the restraints put upon us by our civilization."

–Franz Boas, from the foreward to *Coming of Age in Samoa*

Margaret had found in Samoa, she wrote, a society where life was casual and easy. "The Samoan background, which makes growing up so easy, so simple a matter, is the general casualness of the whole society....From the first months of life, when a child is handed carelessly from one woman's hands to another's, the lesson is learned of not caring for one person greatly, not setting high hopes on any one relationship." In the United States, personal and family tensions were always at their greatest during the teenage years. By contrast, Margaret called adolescence in Samoa "the age of maximum ease." The teenage years for these men and women were free of stress and conflict.

The Extended Family

Margaret credited the lack of tension in Samoa to the system of raising children, which took place in extended families of fifteen or twenty related people. In this system, no one had a special claim to a particular child. The child "belonged" to the group, not to its parents. This means that it was not negatively influenced, as sometimes happens elsewhere, by having unloving parents. Nor was it spoiled by parents who were too indulgent. In Samoa, there was always someone in the extended family to give a child affection.

The idea of the small family (often referred to as the "nuclear family")—each member dependent on the others—has always been important to North Americans. It is not surprising that Margaret's praise of Samoan society brought her criticism in the United States. The criticism, however, was not entirely about praising a different family structure. It also had a great deal to do with teenage sexual conduct. The easy, friendly warmth of the Samoan extended-family spread also, Margaret observed, into the sexual lives of Samoan

"We are all accustomed to consider all those actions that are part and parcel of our own culture, standards which we follow automatically, as common to all mankind. . . . Courtesy, modesty, good manners, conformity to definite ethical standards are universal, but what constitutes courtesy, modesty, good manners, and ethical standards is not universal. It is instructive to know that standards differ in the most unexpected ways. It is still more important to know how the individual reacts to these standards."

–Franz Boas, from the foreward to *Coming of Age in Samoa*

teenagers. Young Samoans thought little of romantic love, only of gaining sexual experience. Because sex was not viewed in the same way as it is in the United States, teenagers having sexual relationships did not create conflict with their families. In the United States, however, teenagers have always been encouraged to save sexual relations until marriage.

Margaret's book offered observations, theories, and ideas that were unsettling to mainstream America.

Because of this, there were some cheap attacks on her private life as well. Some people questioned what kind of young married woman would keep her maiden name and live away from her husband in an uncivilized culture for six months.

"An Outstanding Achievement"

What mattered most to Margaret, however, was the opinion of respected fellow anthropologists. The quality of her field work has been seriously questioned in recent years, but at the time, *Coming of Age in Samoa* was greeted with wild praise. A leading anthropologist, Bronislaw Malinowski, had warned Margaret before she left that she could achieve nothing in such short a time. But later, he admitted his mistake and called her book an "outstanding achievement."

Perhaps the greatest triumph of Margaret's book was that it brought an understanding to the public. Despite its lofty scientific ambitions, *Coming of Age in Samoa* was, and still is, a very readable book. For the first time, ordinary people who were not scholars could connect to anthropology. Margaret's study of the way family and kinship relationships varied among different peoples gave readers new ways to look at themselves, as well as the people around them.

The 1920s stereotype of American family life: father—"the breadwinner"— goes off to business, leaving his wife to look after the home and children.

New Guinea

By the time she read the reviews for her book, Margaret was already at work in New Guinea. In October 1928 she had married Reo Fortune in New Zealand, and they had sailed on to the Admiralty Islands, located off the northeast coast of New Guinea.

The Admiralty Islands is a group of about 40 islands, of which Manus is the largest. From 1885 to 1914 the islands had been occupied by Germany. After World War I, they were administered by Australia. Some islanders had been known to be cannibals and head-hunters.

Margaret and Reo based themselves in Peri, on the island of Manus. This field trip was far more pleasant for Margaret than her first. She not only had her husband's companionship and love, but also the opportunity to discuss her work with him. She had the added benefit of his skilled photography, something she lacked. Her own photographs of Samoa had been out of focus, smudged, and badly composed.

This young girl (above) from the Enga tribe, and the tribesman (opposite) are both in traditional costume. They reflect the kind of culture Margaret found in New Guinea.

Manus contrasted sharply from Samoa. The people lived in houses built on stilts above the waters of a lagoon. They had never been visited by missionaries or traders. No foreigner had landed there until 1875, and few had landed since. The islanders knew nothing of the outside world. Their lives revolved around the monthly flow of tides over the reef. This brought the water that provided them with fish.

Unlike Samoa, there was no easygoing approach to life here. The people of Manus were great worriers. If they did anything that their superstition considered wrong—which could mean something as trivial as gossiping or accidently brushing against a member of the opposite sex—they believed that ghosts would come in the night and punish them by damaging their houses or boats, or spoiling their fish catch. There was no singing or dancing in the evening. Teenage girls were kept strictly indoors. Sexual relationships were not talked about.

Bringing Up Toddlers

Margaret's real interest on the trip was observing the children under five. As before, she was concerned with figuring out how much of a child's capabilities for life are inherited and how much it absorbs from the community as it grows up—the question of nature vs. nurture.

While the people of the 1920s were grappling with nature vs. nurture, they were also witnessing the growth of "progressive education." This approach was based on the belief that children are naturally creative. They learn best, according to progressive educationists, when they are given freedom to learn what they want at their own pace.

In many ways, this was the nature argument. If it was correct, then the Manus children, who were

Death ceremonies featured effigies of the dead, like this one photographed by Reo Fortune at Kenakatem on the Yuat River.

left to play throughout their childhood, should have been full of invention and creativity. In fact, they were nothing like that. Margaret found their play pointless and repetitive, and they seemed to learn nothing from it. They didn't even seem to enjoy it very much.

The apparent "dullness" of their lives continued as they grew. The adults appeared to focus solely on work. They did not care about art, storytelling, music, dance, or even friendship. Life seemed to have little meaning for them apart from their need to survive.

Margaret felt that the "emptiness" of the lives of the people of Manus sprang from the fact that their elders took little interest in them as children. Adults, in general, set no example of how to appreciate the more exciting aspects of life. In other words, the quality of children's lives, and their later lives as adults, depended upon adult input and role-modeling when they were young— in other words: nurture.

"Mr. Margaret Mead"

Back in New York in 1929, Reo worked on his study of Manus religion, while Margaret returned to her job at the American Museum of Natural History.

Reo had been an admirable colleague of Margaret's in New Guinea. But in New York, their relationship began to show signs of stress. He had been brought up in New Zealand. There, old-fashioned Victorian ideas of the way men and women behaved were still common. He seemed out of place in the more modern life of New York. Margaret complained that he made no attempt to help with the housework, and at the same time resented the time she gave to it.

Coming of Age in Samoa had made Margaret's professional reputation. Reo remained unknown.

"If the children's imaginations are to flourish, they must be given food. Although the exceptional children may create something of their own, the great majority of children do not even imagine fear-inspiring bears under the bed unless the adult provides the bears."

—Franz Boas, from the foreward to *Coming of Age in Samoa*

He joked uneasily that he should be introduced to Margaret's friends as "Mr. Margaret Mead."

Meanwhile, there were other worries. The Great Depression of 1929 had crippled the United States economy. Many people lost their savings. Their jobs disappeared, too, as company after company went out of business. Margaret's pay at the American Museum of Natural History, already small, was cut. There was talk of another world war.

Margaret and Reo now planned to go back to New Guinea. In the meantime, Margaret's new book, *Growing Up in New Guinea*, had been published and was widely praised. There was, however, one harsh reviewer who said that Margaret had not understood the kinship of family organization systems in Manus. She was furious at this criticism

and delayed their return to New Guinea for three months while she wrote an academic paper defending herself.

Margaret—almost thirty—and Reo sailed for New Guinea in September 1931. Their study this time was to be of the mountain folk of Arapesh, the river-dwellers of Mundugumor, and also the lake-dwellers of Tchambuli—three of the most primitive and isolated societies in the world.

The Roles of Men and Women

Margaret's mother had been an early feminist. Perhaps her mother's beliefs influenced Margaret's next choice of subject. Reo's attitude toward his wife may have also played a part. Margaret wanted to see how and why the men and women of

primitive societies organized their male and female roles. Were some activities considered naturally male or female, or was this decided by custom and tradition? Again, this went to the very heart of the nature or nurture question.

In Arapesh, the split between Margaret and Reo grew wider. She accepted the people, but Reo could not relate to them. He became infuriated with their servant boys and would threaten to hit them. Margaret would have to step in. "Reo came," she wrote later, "from a culture in which boys were physically disciplined and men beat women, whereas I came from a family tradition within which probably no man had lifted a hand to strike a wife or child in several generations."

Three More Cultures

The Arapesh were difficult to talk to, and Margaret began to feel depressed. Nothing much happened there, and so there was little on which to base any research. On top of it all, her second marriage was falling apart. The hostile review of *Growing Up in New Guinea* still stung her. The eight months in Arapesh were one of the low points in her life.

In 1932, Reo and Margaret moved to the Yuat River and began living near the Mundugumor people. There was "a fierce group of cannibals" in the area who had a history of raiding nearby villages and carrying off the women. "Reo decided that this time he would do the culture and I would do the language, the children, and the technology." But they could find only one person who had any sound information. "It was extraordinarily hard and unrewarding work."

Mundugumor men and women alike were fierce, possessive, and rejected the idea of warmth and affection. Women wanted sons and men wanted daughters, and live newborn babies of the "wrong" sex were thrown into the river. Not surprisingly, Margaret reacted to all this with horror. She became increasingly agitated when she saw that Reo had some sympathy with this culture, a culture whose traditions she found disturbing.

When they left the Yuat River just before Christmas in 1932, both Reo and Margaret were despondent. Their field work had been thin and disappointing. They needed, they felt, to try again somewhere else in New Guinea. They had read about the work of Gregory Bateson, a prominent British anthropologist who was studying the Iatmul people further along the New Guinea coast. There was an unwritten rule that one researcher did not invade another's field, but Margaret and Reo met Gregory Bateson hoping that he could point them in a new direction.

Bateson took them to Aimbom Lake. It was said to be the most beautiful lake in New Guinea. There were about 500 Tchambuli people, living there in three small villages. Almost nothing was known about them. They seemed an ideal subject for study.

There could be no greater difference than the one between the Mundugumor way of life and that of the Tchambuli. The lake-dwelling Tchambuli loved music, dancing, acting, and putting on festivals. They were a stark contrast to the cold, unemotional Mundugumor.

This made for an interesting time, but for Margaret there was something even more interesting. The roles of the Tchambuli men and women were the exact opposite of those in American society. It was the women who were the managers, organizers, and major workers. Meanwhile, the men devoted much of their time to artistic activities like carving, painting, and dancing. The men met in their own clubhouses to carry on these

Margaret Mead with her third husband, Gregory Bateson.

Different, but strikingly similar displays of male adornment from opposite sides of the world: above left, a punk in a London street; above right: a New Guinea man in a head-dress of birds' feathers.

activities, and the women kept away. It was the women who ran the society, and the men were happy to let them. Margaret wrote that, "what the women will think, what the women will do, lies at the back of each man's mind." She did not need to point out the differences in the United States.

Margaret and Reo Part

While Reo and Margaret stayed with the Tchambuli, Gregory Bateson worked in a nearby village. The three spent a lot of time together. Gregory knew the local language well, and Margaret was glad to use him as a sounding-board for her ideas. Gradually, she found that she was turning to him more often than to her husband Reo. "By then," Margaret wrote later, "Gregory and I had already established a kind of communication in which Reo did not share."

It was as it had been with Margaret, Luther, and Reo five years before, when a more interesting and sympathetic man filled the void left by a failing marriage. When the three left New Guinea in the spring of 1933, they each went their separate ways. Margaret sailed for New York, Reo for New Zealand, and Gregory for England. It was clear, however, that Margaret's second marriage was over, and that her third would be to Gregory.

"Wasteful" Roles

The field work among the Arapesh, the Mundugmor, and the Tchambuli was the basis of Margaret's third book, *Sex and Temperament in Three Primitive Societies*, published in 1935.

By now, people expected a Margaret Mead book to contain challenging ideas. The notion that men and women need not necessarily adopt the roles given to them in Western society delighted feminists. The traditional female role of mother, Margaret wrote, was "wasteful of the gifts of many women who could exercise other functions far better than their ability to bear children in an already overpopulated world." The traditional male role was "wasteful of the gifts of many men who could exercise their special personality gifts far better in the home than in the marketplace." Margaret was again raising questions about the accepted pattern of American society where men were breadwinners and women were homemakers. Many Americans resented what they saw as an attack on basic family structure.

Blue Eyes or Brown?

Margaret asked whether classifying people by their sex made anymore sense than classifying them by whether their eyes are blue or brown. Society might just as easily decide that, for example, all

> "Field work is a very difficult thing to do. To do it well, one has to sweep one's mind clear of every presupposition, even those about other cultures in the same part of the world in which one is working. . . . In the field one can take nothing for granted."
>
> —Margaret Mead, from her autobiography *Blackberry Winter*

blue-eyed people were "gentle homemakers" and all brown-eyed people were "strong breadwinners." But that way some people would be forced into roles to which they were not suited. In the same way, Margaret suggested, many men and women in Western society, whose temperaments varied greatly, were forced into roles in which they did not fit.

Some readers misunderstood what Margaret was saying. Just as they had thought that her first book was endorsing the sexual habits of young Samoans, critics now charged that she was also denying any true difference between the sexes. As an anthropologist, Margaret simply wanted to analyze and report on how different peoples organized their societies. Her purpose was to explore what could be learned by her findings.

When she wrote her book, Margaret was well aware that the questions she was asking were relevant to her own personal life. When she had been engaged to Luther Cressman, she had planned to have a large family. Medical problems, she thought, had put an end to that dream. She had kept her interest in children and was happiest when she was working with them. But, as she wrote later, "my own interest in children did not fit the stereotype of the American career woman or, for that matter, the stereotype of the possessive, managing American wife and mother."

A Third Marriage, and Bali

Margaret and Reo were divorced in July of 1935. Margaret, who was in New York, and Gregory, in Cambridge, began to plan a field trip that they could take together as husband and wife. They chose Bali, one of the string of islands in the Indian Ocean that make up what is now called Indonesia. At the time, it was a Dutch colony.

This trip was to be very different from the earlier ones. Bali was a land of more than one million people who spoke the same language. There were a few hundred languages in the New Guinea cultures that Margaret had studied.

This coming of age ceremony marked a young Balinese girl's official entry into adulthood.

Balinese art and culture were already well known in the United States. A large number of Europeans and Americans lived on the island. There were dancers, artists, musicians, writers, and people who were there to observe and enjoy the Balinese arts. There would be none of the isolation of previous field trips. And there would be

This was called the "mosquito room" in the house Margaret and Gregory built in the Balinese village of Bajoeng Gede. It enabled them to work late, with the lights on, protected by netting from mosquitoes.

no hurry. Margaret and Gregory planned to stay in Bali for two years.

They were married in Singapore on March 13, 1936, and went to Bali on a slow boat that went from island to island. This was the best-equipped field trip Margaret had ever taken. It was also the first time she would use movie film. She and Gregory had the latest cameras and their own developing and printing equipment. As an added bonus, Gregory's photography was of professional standard. They had no recording equipment of their

own, but they borrowed some from a musician who was on the island studying Balinese music.

"A Paradise"

The newlyweds arrived in Bali at the end of April. For Margaret, Bali was magical. "What a paradise Bali was for us." she wrote. "Ceremonies every day—if not in this village, then in another. . . . Informants, scribes, secretaries. . . . household help too, and when we came home at midnight, dinner would be waiting, hot and delicious."

"We were never again, after the silence of our first day [on Bali], out of the sound of music, if it was only the tinkle of the bells that the women fastened to their knives or the flute played by some lonely peasant watching over his crops in a far field."

—Margaret Mead, from her autobiography *Blackberry Winter*

"Here in a mountain village Mead also had the first and only real home she was ever to have, a house built of pavilions joined by covered walks and furniture made by Balinese craftsmen. After the rigors of New Guinea everything seemed to be accomplished with miraculous ease. At night it was romantically lit by tiny glass lamps."

—Phyllis Grosskurth, from *Margaret Mead. A Life of Controversy*

The richness of Balinese culture astonished and delighted them. There were shadow plays featuring puppets reflected against a thin screen under a swinging light. There were traditional costumes and markings, orchestral concerts, Balinese operas, and great feasts.

"We responded to it," wrote Margaret, "by working at a fever pitch." The valuable result of the two years in Bali included more than 28,000 photographs, collections of paintings, carvings, children's drawings and shadow-play puppets, and countless reels of movie film. Most valuable of all, Margaret and Gregory worked out a system of reference and cross-indexing that could identify where each item came from, who was singing and dancing, the names of the people in the background, or the musical instrument being played.

The Clouds of War

From Bali, Margaret and Gregory returned to New Guinea for one year. Before they left in March 1938, she and Gregory had made plans for an ambitious expedition. It would cover a number of sciences that fell broadly under the "umbrella" of anthropology. There would be an educational organization that would teach members of the expedition Balinese language and culture.

By now it was 1939. Hitler's armies were on the march in Europe. It was clear that another world war was not far away. On the ship that took Margaret and Gregory home, British passengers were talking about being called up to fight. Gregory, who was British, felt that it was his duty to return to Britain if the war broke out. Although it was to be two more years before the United States came into World War II, many people— including Margaret—felt that once the war started it would engulf the world.

It was no time to be planning future field trips or setting up a field headquarters in Bali. During World War II, Bali was occupied by Japanese troops. If Margaret and Gregory had been there, they would have certainly been arrested and sent to prison camps.

The direct result of the Bali field trip was *Balinese Character*, produced jointly with Gregory and illustrated with over 700 of the 28,000 photographs. It was intended not only to be a record of their field trip, but also as a model of how research findings in the field could be presented. They also put together four twenty-five-minute films on aspects of Balinese life.

A Baby Arrives

Meanwhile, Margaret had something else to think about. She was pregnant. More than fifteen years previous, she was told she could never have a child. Since then, she had suffered a number of miscarriages. Now, she was overjoyed. But caution

"Before the birth of her baby Margaret had declared that she would assume complete care of the child for the first six months, but within a fortnight, she realized that she couldn't be Super Mom, hold down a job at the Museum, nurse the baby, and be up at all hours of the night."

–Phyllis Grosskurth, from *Margaret Mead. A Life of Controversy*

Margaret with her daughter Catherine, then a few weeks old. The birth of Catherine gave Margaret a new insight into women's lives.

was needed. She was thirty-eight, an age when the birth of a first child is likely to be difficult, if not dangerous. She was advised to take things easy.

Margaret had by now been a student of child development for most of her adult life. On her field trips she had seen the birth of many babies. Yet, she found that she was just as prone as any first-time mother to worries about her child. She checked her family's history for health problems. She remembered that some of her relatives were prone to deafness. Yet, she saw the forthcoming birth as an interesting event from the professional as well as personal point of view. She even went as far as arranging for a friend to film it. When the time came, Margaret worked to slow down the birth so that the friend could change flash bulbs right in the middle!

Mary Catherine Bateson, known to the family as Cathy, was born on December 8, 1939, three

Margaret Mead studies an exhibit at the American Museum of Natural History, where she held a series of appointments from 1926 until her death in 1978.

months after World War II broke out. "Bringing up Cathy," Margaret wrote, "was an intellectual as well as emotionally exciting adventure." It was an opportunity for her to put into practice her ideas from years of observation of parents and children. But she knew that there was a danger in this. Cathy ran the risk of being seen more as a live piece of field work than a child of loving parents.

Although Margaret had a worldwide reputation as an anthropologist, neither she nor Gregory had been able to save any money. Before Cathy was born, Margaret had done some occasional lecturing. She now returned to this, together with part-time work at the museum in New York.

When the United States entered the war in 1941, there was plenty of work for experts who had studied the problems of change in people's lives. For Americans joining the forces, for wives and children left home, and for women drafted into war work, World War II was the biggest change that could be imagined. Both Margaret and Gregory were in demand for ideas on helping people cope with problems of separation and new experiences. But this was not an anthropological field of work, which Margaret felt to be the core of her life. And while the war went on, there was no chance of returning to the South Pacific.

Into the Field Again

It was June 1953 before Margaret felt free to return to field work. By now, she was divorced from Gregory and Cathy was thirteen years old.

There had been great upheavals in the South Pacific since Margaret was last there in 1939. Great movements of thousands of Japanese and American troops through the islands had changed the way of life there forever. It had also changed the ideas of many of the native people.

"Mead was thoroughly at home in New York. She had her secure job at the Museum of Natural History, a wide network of supportive friends, and the status of a national celebrity. Bateson was just as hungry for recognition as his wife, but there was not way he could compete with her. 'It was almost a principle of pure energy,' he recalled ruefully. 'I couldn't keep up and she couldn't stop.'"

–Phyllis Grosskurth, from *Margaret Mead. A Life of Controversy*

"In these years her appearance became more and more schoolmarmish—something the American public seemed to like. What mattered most to her was energy, and the house was bursting with noise—people constantly coming and going, and talk over the table long after dinner was finished."

–Phyllis Grosskurth, from *Margaret Mead. A Life of Controversy*

A sand painting from New Guinea.

Most of the islands of Indonesia were still under the control of European countries, Australia, or the United States. After the war ended, a number of independence movements sprang up. In 1949, the Dutch government eventually gave independence to a string of islands that made up Indonesia. Bali was free.

These events altered the character of the places Margaret had known well in the 1930s. One change in particular was for the better. Since the 1930s, new equipment had been developed that helped with field work. There were portable electric generators, new photographic lighting—and, most valuable of all, the portable tape recorder. It was no longer necessary—as it had been in Bali before World War II—to use cumbersome equipment with poor quality sound and limited recording time. Cameras, too, had improved.

Although field work in the 1950s was more difficult in some ways, at least it was done with better equipment. Added to this was the advantage of increased ease and speed of travel. It was important to Margaret, who had a child at home, that a trip that once took two months twenty years earlier, now only took two days.

The World in a "Saucer"

For her first post-war trip, Margaret Mead, age fifty-one, chose to return to the village of Peri in Manus in the Admiralty Islands, which she had last seen in 1929. She was interested in the changes that had taken place, and wanted to find out how the villagers had reacted to them.

But Margaret soon to realized that changes in Manus went far beyond anything she could have imagined on her earlier trip.

In the 1920s, the people of Peri had no knowledge of anything outside their village. Their picture

Above: *A Roman Catholic church in New Guinea.*

Left: *A "western-style" New Guinea classroom. Margaret felt that Western ideas had been imported to the islands without enough thought about the impact they would have on the people.*

"Which is harder for them to assimilate and understand—a savage way of life, which in so many respects is like that of their grandfathers, now so enthusiastically abandoned, or a way of life which belongs to the modern world, the world of planes that fly overhead and news that comes over the radio?"

—Margaret Mead, writing from Peri in 1965, from *Letters from the Field*

of the world was "as a giant saucer, and the waters of the sea slopping up and away on every side." The passage of time was marked by the monthly flow of water over the reef. They knew nothing of their history except for stories of things that had happened in their parents' or grandparents' lifetime.

The changes had started soon after Margaret left Manus in 1929. When she was there, the people had not heard of Christianity. Shortly after her departure, Roman Catholic missionaries arrived and converted the Manus people. This brought them some basic education, but the mission schools mainly taught Bible stories.

During World War II, Manus and the rest of the Admiralty Islands had been occupied by the Japanese. In 1946, American forces landed and recaptured them. After a period of American occupation, the islands were returned to Australian control.

This rapid chain of events would have caused upheaval on even the most advanced countries. To the people of the small island of Manus, it seemed as if their world had been turned upside-down two or three times.

Manus had been a base for transporting troops to and from the Far East. Margaret estimated that over one million white men had passed through the island. This was an astonishing experience for the people who, only a few years before, had virtually no contact with the outside world.

Wonder and Envy

The people of Manus looked with wonder, not only at the soldiers, but at their equipment—aircraft, bulldozers, searchlights, torpedo boats. The young people looked with envy as well as wonder. They saw how a bulldozer with one driver could do as much work in one day as a team of Manus men using hand tools could only do in months. They enjoyed the canned food and other goods that were showered upon them by American soldiers.

The young people decided that they would make changes. No more back-breaking work with hand tools. No more old-fashioned ceremonies organized by old men of the village, locked into the poor and hopeless past.

The American troops went home, leaving behind stores of canned food and other things that were immensely valuable to villagers who had lived all their lives on the edge of poverty. Corrugated iron, plywood, metal shelving, canvas sheeting, chairs, tables, paraffin lamps—the list of abandoned items was endless. Inevitably, these stocks eventually ran out.

A New Manus

When Margaret revisited Manus in 1953, the local people were wearing Western clothes. In Peri, the houses over the lagoon had been demolished and new houses, with European-style kitchens and windows, were built on shore, although still on

The group at the bottom was photographed in Manus in 1928. Second from the right is John Kilipak, then a thirteen-year-old cookboy.

Below: *Kilipak in 1953, when Margaret returned.*

stilts. Scrap drums left behind by the Americans were used to store water. New villages had been built and each one had a central square, which served as a meeting place. Councils were created, each with an elected leader. There were other plans for improvements—but only plans, because there was no money to turn them into reality. The building of hospitals, clinics, schools, and banks would have to wait.

During the American occupation, the islands had seen a different kind of society at work. "They were caught up in the spectacle of so many people all alike, the great scale of the army barracks, the bulldozer constructions, and the great planes." They envied and admired the way Americans behaved. "They contrasted their own endless quarreling over a single broken clay pot and the American willingness to spend any amount of money, time, and equipment to save the life of a single soldier." They also noted that black American troops were dressed, housed, and paid as well as the white people. "They felt that the Americans had made the 'men of Africa all right.'"

Progress, but . . .

The new lifestyle that the Manus people achieved after the war was somewhat shortlived. It had been made by using dumped American materials, all of which had been used up by 1953.

In her writing, Margaret expressed that the Manus people were racing ahead of themselves. "Their imaginative grasp of the possibilities of modernity," she reported, "outruns their resources. They understand how to tell time and set a meeting for 'one o'clock.' But there are only two clocks and one watch in the village, and the meeting is less likely to start on time than when meetings were set by the sun. They have also learned about

"And in her flowing cape and with the forked cherrywood stick that [Margaret Mead] now carried with her everywhere, she spoke and looked like a prophet, a role she found particularly satisfying. Americans liked her for being fat and plain. People frequently told her that she reminded them of their mothers."

–Phyllis Grosskurth, from *Margaret Mead. A Life of Controversy*

dates, but they have no calendar, so what day it is a matter of protracted discussion—or it was until I arrived. They want good materials and good equipment, but they cannot write to order it, they do not have any way of sending money."

It was not for Margaret Mead to judge whether the changes she had seen in Manus were a good or bad thing, though she had—like many people—a sentimental regret for the vanishing past. Most of the adults she spoke to on Manus in 1953 had been children when she was there in 1929. They had grown up in a world of superstition, fear, and poverty.

Margaret's return trip to Manus was an eye-opening experience for her in many ways. Clearly, it marked a significant change in her professional interests. Previously, she had been interested mainly in the natural changes that happened in communities. Now, she was forced to investigate the results of huge changes that had happened suddenly because of the war. These changes had led to a transition within the community. From 1953 on, she became most interested and active in helping the Western world to understand the need for change in under-developed countries. She wanted to educate people about how money and technical aid could best be used.

Winding Down

The return to Manus was the last field trip on which Margaret did most of the work herself. She was now over fifty. Even with the convenience of modern travel, conditions in remote places were harsh and challenging. Margaret now needed to satisfy her thirst for field work by maintaining regular correspondence with friends and students who were working in the same territory, though often with other interests.

. . . .

"What is there for young anthropologists to do? In one sense, everything. The best possible work has not yet been done. If I were twenty-one today I would elect to join the communicating network of those young people, the world over, who recognize the urgency of life-supporting change— as an anthropologist."

—Margaret Mead, from her autobiography *Blackberry Winter*

. . . .

In 1954, Margaret revisited the Manus village of Peri, where she had worked in 1928. She admired the new school and the way it had "opened the doors to the world" for the Manus children, but she worried that education would tempt young people to move away, leaving only the old and sick in the village.

In 1960, Margaret's daughter Catherine married. Margaret now found herself with much more time to devote to her work again. Between 1964 and 1975, she made several trips around the world to visit field workers who were past acquaintances. She was also writing and editing a steady stream of books, holding a number of part-time academic posts, and was in demand as a speaker at national and international conferences.

Margaret went back to Manus again in 1964 and visited with Lokus, who was a "houseboy" in the residence where she and Reo had lived in 1928. When she visited in 1953, he had been a cook in the house of a friend. Now, age fifty or so, he was chief cook in charge of a household. He remembered small details from her first visit. "Every event," she wrote home, "is tied firmly into the shared past."

In the eleven years since she had last visited, progress had made another giant leap forward. Over thirty Manus children had gone on to some form of higher education outside the village—as students, teachers, or nurses. "The new education has opened the doors to the world," Margaret wrote, but it also had a sad side. The Manus girls who had been away and had come back were treated as "damaged goods." No one wanted to marry them because it was not thought right for girls to travel among strangers.

Questions About Samoa

By 1932, concrete plans to combat the Great Depression were finally being put into place. With the election of Franklin Roosevelt as president, a new mood of hope spread throughout the United States. Programs for full employment, social security, and better education—known collectively as the New Deal—were set up. The atmosphere was one in which new ideas flourished and were welcomed—Margaret Mead's included.

By the end of World War II in 1945, the mood had changed. As individuals and as a nation, Americans were now terrified by the spread of Communism. Liberal thinkers, actors, film directors, writers, and academics like Margaret Mead came—quite unjustly—under suspicion. Some accused her and others of undermining the "American way of life." After 1953, this may have been part of the reason Margaret decided to spend time in the field again, away from the disturbing politics at home.

But a bigger storm was brewing. It involved a New Zealand anthropologist, Derek Freeman, who had been researching in Western Samoa since 1940. At first a follower of Margaret Mead and the nurture school of thought, he gradually came to

"I bring my own life to throw what light it may on how children can be brought up so that parents and children, together, can weather the roughest seas."

–Margaret Mead, from her autobiography *Blackberry Winter*

"Mead became the center of attention at interdisciplinary conferences, TV interviews, and lecture engagements (sixty or so a year). Wherever she went she took with her a small silk pillow which allowed her to drop asleep on planes or in hotel rooms. One colleague remarked that when one entered a restaurant, Mead's voice could be heard above all the rest, her face growing ruddier with the passing years."

–Phyllis Grosskurth, from *Margaret Mead. A Life of Controversy*

51

Today in Pago Pago, market traders make their sales pitches to the tourists, but the goods they are selling—like those in the picture—have very little in common with the early culture of the people.

question her findings and her methods of research. By the time he left Samoa in November 1943, he knew that he would one day have to publicly question the picture of Samoan life that Margaret Mead had presented, as well as the methods she had used to gather her data.

In 1964, Derek Freeman met Margaret Mead and, in a long private conversation, told her of his views. This was the start of a long correspondence during the next ten years. He was not the only critic of Margaret's picture of Samoa. In the 1970s, she met Samoan university students in the United States and Australia who asked her to revise her Samoa book. She refused, writing (in the preface of her new edition) that *Coming of Age in Samoa* was "true to what I saw in Samoa and what I was able to convey of what I saw, true to the state of our knowledge of human behavior as it was in the mid-1920s."

By 1978, Derek Freeman had finished a draft of his book, which he offered to send Margaret for comment. She did not reply, and a few months later, on November 15, she died—a month before her 77th birthday.

Was Margaret Mead Right?

Derek Freeman's book, *Margaret Mead and Samoa*, was published in the United States in 1983. It caused an immediate sensation.

Coming of Age in Samoa was, and still is, the best-selling anthropological book of all time. Generations of students—including Derek Freeman himself—had been taught to see it as a model of anthropological research. But, according to him, it was flawed and hollow.

Margaret had spent only ten weeks learning the Samoan language, as she had admitted. This meant, Derek Freeman said, that she could have only had a brief and very basic understanding of how to communicate when she began to interview her sample of Samoan girls. She had chosen to live in the household of a U. S. Navy family, the Holts. This, according to Freeman, would have identified her as part of the naval government that many Samoans both feared and resented. Instead of interviewing the Samoan girls in their homes in their own villages, they were called to the European-style navy house.

Not a Paradise On Earth

For these reasons and others, Derek Freeman argued that Margaret had never found out the true cultural influences and way of life in Samoa. It was far from being the peaceful "paradise on earth" that she had described, where there was no hatred or tension and where the happy natives lived only to love. Samoa was, according to Freeman, a violent society. As for the "free love" Margaret attributed to them, Samoans followed—and, if necessary, enforced—a code of sexual conduct which was as strict as in most American communities. It was the picture of themselves as sexually casual that had upset Samoans the most.

Freeman suggested that Margaret's Samoan informants had teased her with stories about "casual love under the palm trees." He pointed out that Margaret, age twenty-three and slight in stature, was smaller than some of the girls she was interviewing and that, as she wrote, they treated her as "one of themselves." They may have used the interviews mostly to brag about their boyfriends, not to give an accurate account of their lives.

Freeman's conclusion was that Margaret's work on Samoa was accepted uncritically by Franz Boas and his colleagues because it agreed with their own theories.

Fact or Fiction?

Nothing in Margaret's later work attracted very much criticism, but Derek Freeman's book put a question mark over her whole career. There is now no way of knowing if what she reported from Samoa in 1925 was true. Anthropology is not a science of pure facts.

A chemist knows that if you expose a piece of iron to moist air, a layer of iron oxide, or rust, will form on the surface of the iron. It always happens like that, and it is always iron oxide, not some other chemical compound, that forms. But anthropology is concerned with observing the patterns of how human beings behave. They don't always behave in the same way—and they are not always observed in the same way.

....

"I have yet to meet a Samoan who agrees with Mead's assertion that adolescence in Samoan society is smooth, untroubled and unstressed.... Adolescents would tell us of the tensions between themselves and their parents, and of their emotional distress during altercations with their families or when they were heavily dominated by someone in authority."

–Derek Freeman, from *Margaret Mead and Samoa*

....

It may be quite true that Margaret Mead got some things wrong. We can only trust her word that *Coming of Age in Samoa* is a true and accurate record of what she saw. But even if the picture she gave of Samoa in the 1920s is faulty, the book is still valuable in other ways. It shows in detail how field work was done at the time. It shows how families and society far away from modern influences organized themselves. And Margaret wrote about the way humans behave in a manner that gave us a vocabulary for understanding our own families and communities.

Out of the Museum

Anthropology began in the nineteenth century. Exploration and settlement in other parts of the world had shown the wide variety of cultures that exist on Earth. Anthropology was concerned with how different races and groups adapted to their environments, how they pictured the whole world, and how their language and their arts—that is, their culture—reflected their ideas.

Until early in the twentieth century, only a few people knew the details of the discoveries and theories of anthropologists. And even fewer had seen examples of different arts and crafts that were collected in the field.

Nineteenth-century anthropologists tended to treat people they were studying as specimens. Subjects were observed in a formal, clinical, and prescribed way, through the eyes of nineteenth-century Western intellectuals. Little attempt was made to get inside the minds of people or to see their points of view.

Margaret Mead was revolutionary in the way she combined the academic approach with a more human view of research. She drew up enormous tables of kinship showing the relationships of the

"We are thus confronted in the case of Margaret Mead's Samoan researches with an instructive example of how, as evidence is sought to substantiate a cherished doctrine, the deeply held beliefs of those involved may lead them unwittingly into error."

–Derek Freeman, from *Margaret Mead and Samoa*

55

"There is hope, I believe, in seeing the human adventure as a whole and in the shared trust that knowledge about mankind, sought in reverence for life, can bring life."

—Margaret Mead,
from her autobiography
Blackberry Winter

villagers she studied, and kept careful records of the important details of their lives. But she also treated the villagers as individuals with their own stories to tell. She was intensely interested in, and sympathetic to, people as human beings, not merely as objects in her study. This gave her writing a vitality that appealed to readers from all backgrounds, especially non-academics.

Some credit Margaret Mead as the person who brought anthropology out of the museum drawer and made an understanding of cultural diversity available to everyone.

"Stories Told and Retold"

Margaret Mead did not invent such terms as kinship groups, taboos, and other anthropological expressions that are commonly used today. But the fact that they are so widely used and understood is due mainly to her writing. By reading her accounts of primitive cultures, the ways in which people relate to one another become clearer.

Above and opposite:
Weddings are a universally human ritual that focus and reflect cultural beliefs about the nature and role of the family. The differing details of these three weddings are evidence of how different cultures approach this revered rite of passage.

In a letter written from the field in 1967, Margaret observed that: "It is only through the eyes of intense living in face-to-face relationships that the life and culture of a whole people can be fully experienced. It is through the records of such closely bound lives that we may hope to understand the human need for continuity, repetitive experience, and intimacy. For intimacy has its source in just these familiar repetitions of laughter at old jokes, remembered anger at old quarrels, meals eaten together at the same twilight and children listening to accounts of things that happened before their parents were born, stories told and retold."

Margaret Mead's Gift

The kind of intimacy Margaret Mead wrote about is at the heart of family festivals in all cultures, including Western culture. It was her gift that she could observe and articulate what was at the heart of family celebrations that took place on the other side of the world. In doing so, she showed Westerners that there are more similarities binding human cultures together than there are differences separating them.

Another important aspect of Margaret Mead's work is highlighted by her experiences on her later trips to Peri, where she was able to observe change over three generations. The upheavals caused in Manus by World War II have been mirrored in many countries. Her observations and comments, which were unpopular at the time with many government officials, are relevant to the problems of any underdeveloped country trying to take its place in the modern world today.

Margaret Mead brought anthropology to the forefront of social discussion. Perhaps her most important and long-lasting contribution, however, was her ability to broaden our understanding of ourselves.

She did this by helping to define the many disparate elements that actually combine to make up a culture. And, in defining what culture is, she helped us all to look at how and why we have come to be who we are.

Her methods and her conclusions were, at times, controversial. But, new ideas—especially ones that challenge an established sysytem—are always met with resistance. Margaret Mead's goal was never to be a revolutionary, it was simply to observe and record what she saw. As she wrote in *Coming of Age in Samoa*, she said her hope was to reveal to us all more about how we come develop our identities, "Realizing that our own ways are not humanly inevitable nor God-ordained, but are the fruit of a long and turbulent history, we may well examine in turn all of our institutions, thrown into strong relief against the history of other civilizations, and weighing them in the balance, be not afraid to find them wanting."

In assessing Margaret Mead's true legacy, it should not be forgotten that she was a pioneer for women. When she undertook her career in the 1920s, she was boldly forging a new female role model, not only in science, but in all walks of life. She was also undertaking work that posed serious dangers and hardships, she was engaging the public in frank discussions of sex roles, sexuality, and adolescence. These "delicate" subjects had previously been reserved only for the formal—traditionally male—settings of the academic or medical world. In forging ahead with her work, despite criticism, Margaret Mead laid the foundation for all women of future generations who wished to pursue careers in science.

On Margaret Mead's last visit to Peri in 1975, she was photographed with the widow of the man who had acted as her interpreter forty-seven years before.

The Everlasting Argument

The question of nature vs. nurture was a very important topic in Margaret Mead's research. It's now hard to imagine how, at the beginning of the

From her field trips, Margaret brought back a rich variety of artifacts, some gifts made especially for her, others bought after prolonged bargaining. All the items, she contended, revealed a special aspect of that culture's beliefs.

twentieth century, academics opposed each other so strongly over this very question. It is now generally agreed among most scientists that the way an individual person behaves is partly inherited and partly a direct result of what a person learns as he or she grows up. It may be that further research into DNA (the carrier of hereditary information in the cells that make up the body) will reveal more about nature in the decades to come.

Any scientist knows that it is always dangerous to think that a final answer has been found. In anthropology, as in other disciplines, there is always more to be discovered. Margaret Mead was one of those special individuals who had the courage to point others toward the endless path of discovery.

Important Dates

1901	**Dec 16:** Margaret Mead is born.
1918	Margaret graduates from high school and meets Luther Cressman, her first husband.
1919	Margaret begins studies at DePauw College in Indiana State, but leaves after one year.
1920	Margaret goes to Barnard College, Columbia University, New York.
1923	Margaret gains her master's degree in psychology and chooses anthropology for her doctorate. **Sept:** Margaret marries Luther Cressman.
1925	**Aug:** Margaret arrives in Samoa.
1926	Margaret meets Reo Fortune on her voyage back from Samoa to Europe, where she spends the summer with Luther. She returns to New York to write *Coming of Age in Samoa* and starts work as Assistant Curator of Ethnology at the American Museum of Natural History in New York.
1927	Margaret and Reo meet in Germany and decide to marry.
1928	**Oct:** Margaret and Reo marry in New Zealand and travel to Manus, the largest of the Admiralty Islands. *Coming of Age is Samoa* is published.
1929	Margaret returns to New York and writes *Growing Up in New Guinea*.
1930	Margaret starts field work with Reo among the Omaha Indians.
1931	**Sept:** Margaret and Reo set out for New Guinea and start their field work among the Arapesh. Margaret and Reo move on to the Mundugumor. **Dec:** Margaret meets Gregory Bateson for the first time.
1933	**Feb:** Margaret and Reo start their field work among the Tchambuli. When they leave New Guinea, Margaret and Reo separate. She returns to New York and writes *Sex and Temperament in Three Primitive Societies*.
1935	**July:** Reo and Margaret divorce. She and Gregory Bateson plan a field trip to Bali.
1936	**Mar 13:** Margaret and Gregory marry in Singapore and go on to Bali.
1938	Margaret and Gregory do eight months' field work in Iatmul, New Guinea.
1939	Margaret and Gregory return to New York. Margaret becomes pregnant. World War II begins and continues until 1945. Margaret and Gregory start writing Balinese Character. **Dec 8:** A daughter, Catherine, is born.

1941	Margaret is invited to go to Washington for government war-time work.
1942	*Balinese Character* is published.
1843	Margaret goes to England for a lecture tour.
1952	Margaret goes to Australia for a lecture tour.
1953	Margaret returns to Manus for a visit.
1954	In addition to her work at the American Museum of History, Margaret is appointed Adjunct Professor of Anthropology at Columbia University.
1957	Margaret makes a second field trip to Bali.
1964	Margaret makes a return visit to Manus.
1966	Margaret makes a field trip to Montserrat, West Indies.
1967	Margaret returns to Tambunam, New Guinea.
1972	Margaret's autobiography, *Blackberry Winter*, is published.
1975	Margaret makes a further visit to Manus.
1978	**Nov 15:** Margaret Mead, aged 76, dies.

Glossary

Adolescence The period of growing up between childhood and adulthood.

Anthropology The scientific study of the human race, in particular its origin, physical development, customs, societies, and the way it behaves.

Child development The process of growing and learning.

Extended family   A family group living together that includes grandparents, parents, children, and other close relatives, such as aunts, uncles, and cousins.

Free love Sexual relations without commitment of marriage or any formal or legal obligation.

Illiterate Being unable to read or write.

Intellectual Being able to learn, think, and reason. Also, someone who has a high level of intelligence.

Kinship Human relationship that is based on blood or marriage. Most human societies and social groupings are founded on kinship and strict social customs, rules, and taboos evolved.

Native Belonging by origin or birth to a particular place in the country.

Nature The effects of heredity as an influence on someone's personality.

Nurture The effects of upbringing and the human environment on someone's personality.

Primitive Relating to the early stages of civilization.

Social security Financial help, provided by the state, for those in need—in particular, the elderly, poor, disabled, sick, and unemployed.

Taboo Something that is prohibited by tradition and social custom.

Temperament The way a person acts, feels, and thinks.

Under-developed Relating to a country, one that is poor and in need of aid from richer nations.

For More Information

Books
Catsiglia, Julie. *Margaret Mead* (Pioneers in Change Series). Morristown, NJ: Silver Burdett Press, 1989.

Facchini, Fiorenzo. Rocco Serini (Translator). *Humans: Origins and Evolution* (Beginnings). Chatham, NJ: Raintree Steck Vaughn, 1994.

Hicks, Peter. *The Hidden Past* (Remarkable World). Chatham, NJ: Raintree Steck Vaughn, 1997.

Powell, Jillian. *Body Decoration* (Traditions Around the World). New York, NY: Thomson Learning, 1995.

Weitzman, David. *Great Lives: Human Culture* (Great Lives Series). Old Tappan, NJ: Atheneum, 1995.

Ziesk, Edra. Matina S. Horner (Designer). *Margaret Mead: Anthropologist* (American Women of Achievement). New York, NY: Chelsea House, 1990.

Web Sites
American Museum of Natural History
Tour the museum where Margaret Mead worked. There are many interesting facts and photographs on human culture—www.amph.org/education/index.html

Margaret Mead
Visit the site dedicated to the great scientist and see the awards she won, notes from many of her field trips, and information about her daughter Catherine—www.thomson.com/gale/cwh/mead.htm

Index